Literacy Consultants
DAVID BOOTH • KATHLEEN GOULD LUNDY

Social Studies Consultant
PETER PAPPAS

A Harcourt Achieve Imprint

10801 N. Mopac Expressway
Building # 3
Austin, TX 78759
1.800.531.5015

Steck-Vaughn is a trademark of Harcourt Achieve Inc. registered in the United States of America and/or other jurisdictions. All inquiries should be mailed to: Paralegal Department, 6277 Sea Harbor Drive, Orlando, FL 32887.

Ru'bicon © 2007 Rubicon Publishing Inc.
www.rubiconpublishing.com

All rights reserved. No part of this publication may be reproduced or transmitted in any form or by any means, electronic or mechanical, including photocopying, recording, taping, or any information storage and retrieval system, without permission in writing from the copyright owner.

Project Editor: Kim Koh
Editor: Vicki Low
Art Director: Jen Harvey
Project Designer: Jan-John Rivera

7 8 9 10 11   5 4 3 2 1

Mars Colony
ISBN 13: 978-1-4190-3213-4
ISBN 10:   1-4190-3213-5

Printed in Singapore

PHOTO CREDITS: Openindex: 2-5, 13, 21, 29, 37, 45-47; istockphoto: 13, 37; NASA: 21, 29, 37, 45-46

MARS COLONY

Written by
ROBERT CUTTING

Illustrated by
DHAMINDRA JEEVAN

New London Schools
MS/HS Library

CHANG FAMILY

JENNY CHANG

DEREK CHANG

FICTIONAL CHARACTERS

JENNY CHANG: A 14-year-old girl whose family is one of the first to move to Mars from Earth.

DEREK CHANG: Jenny's 10-year-old brother.

DR. MICHAEL CHANG AND DR. JEAN CHANG: The parents of Jenny and Derek. They are scientists who are part of the first human colony on Mars.

JOHN DARIUS: The general manager of the Mars colony.

DR. MICHAEL CHANG

DR. JEAN CHANG

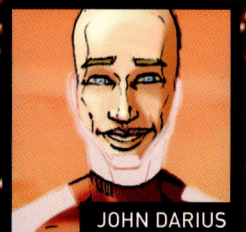
JOHN DARIUS

Contents

4	**Introduction**
6	**Chapter 1: Liftoff!**
13	**Time Out:** Getting to Mars
14	**Chapter 2: A New Home**
21	**Time Out:** Mars Facts and Figures
22	**Chapter 3: The Rescue**
29	**Time Out:** Weather on Mars
30	**Chapter 4: The Secret Revealed**
37	**Time Out:** Life on Mars
38	**Chapter 5: A New Era**
45	**Time Out:** Exploring Mars
46	**Moving On: Mars in Our Future**

INTRODUCTION

Earth

Mars

TIMELINE

1965 »	1971 »	1984 »	1997 »	2001 »
The first spacecraft to visit Mars, *Mariner 4*, sends images back to Earth.	*Mariner 9* maps the whole surface of the planet.	A meteorite from Mars that landed in Antarctica thousands of years ago is found.	The Mars *Pathfinder* lands on Mars.	The Mars Odyssey mission sets out to explore the Martian surface.

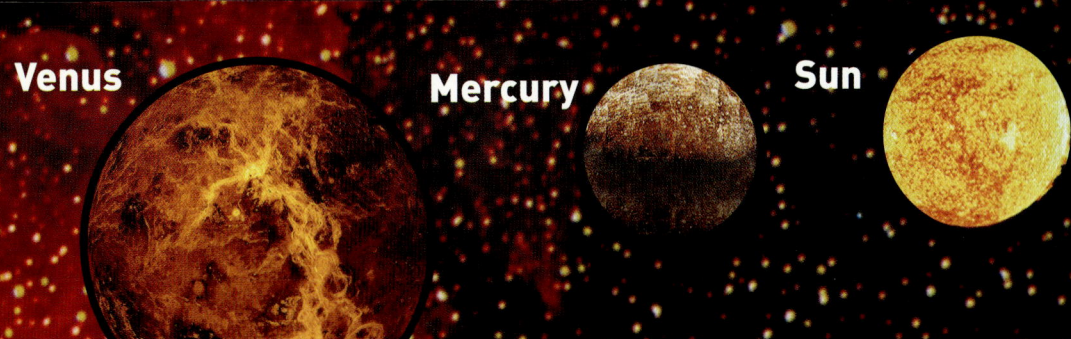

Venus   Mercury   Sun

The planet Mars glows red in the night sky. Is there life on Mars? How could we get there? Could we live there?

Mars is the fourth planet from the sun — after Mercury, Venus, and Earth. Like Earth, it is a hard and rocky planet. We know that there is water on Mars, but much of it is in the form of ice.

People have been observing Mars since the time of the ancient Egyptians. It wasn't until 1964 that we got our first close-up view of the planet from the space probe *Mariner 4*. Since then, other spacecraft have actually landed on Mars, but no human being has gone there yet.

This story is set in an imaginary future. Human beings are arriving on Mars to make a new home for themselves. What will they find when they get there?

WHAT'S THE STORY? This story is set in an imaginary future. The characters and events are fictitious.

2004 »	2005 »	2007 »	2009 »	2011 »
The Mars Rover *Opportunity* lands on Mars to collect rock and soil samples.	A Mars Reconnaissance Orbiter is set to orbit Mars for a full Martian year.	A Mars Lander is scheduled to be launched.	A Mars Science Laboratory Rover is scheduled to be launched.	A Mars Scout Mission is planned to fly to Mars and return with rock and soil samples.

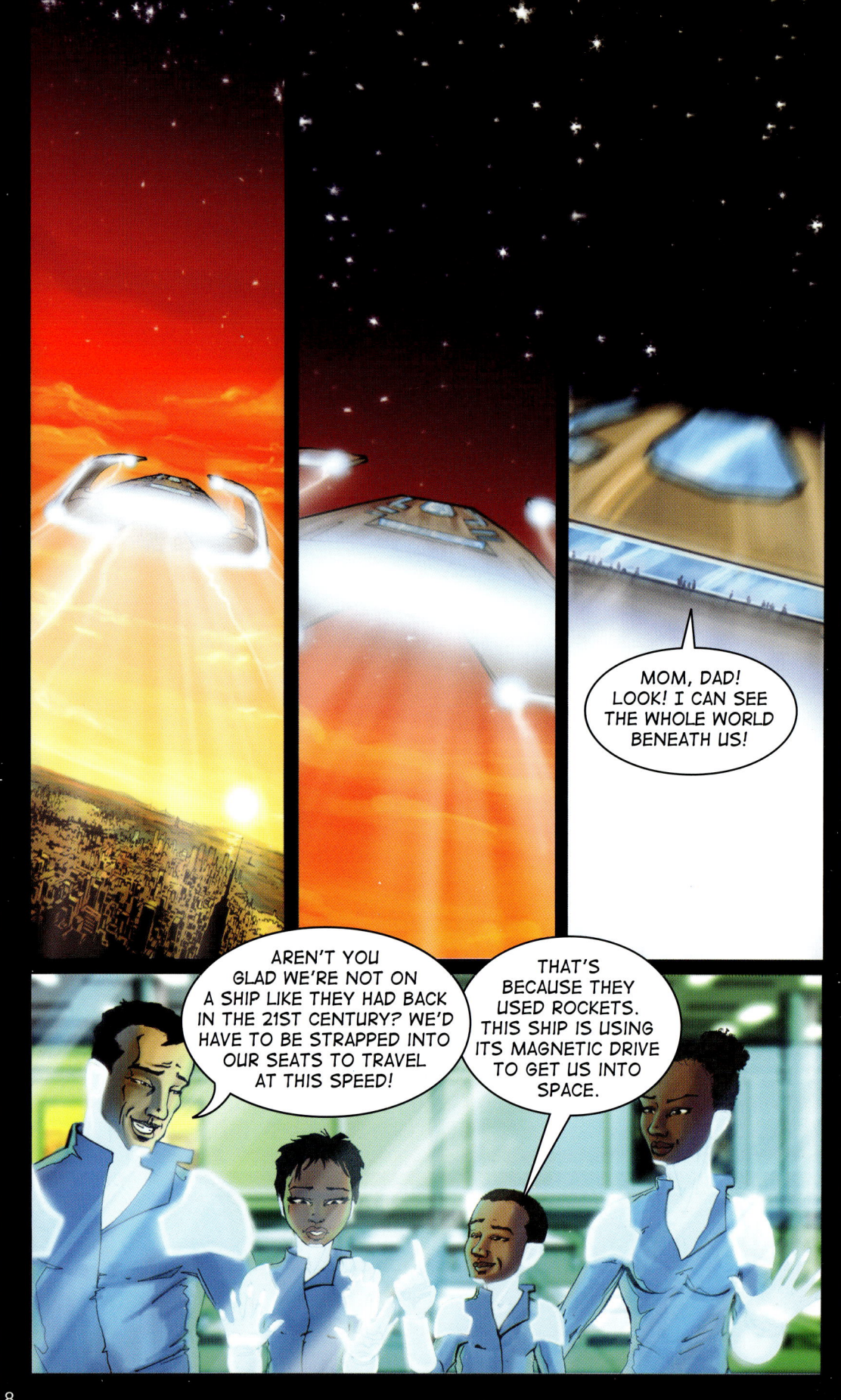

GETTING TO MARS

In our time, spaceships still use jet fuel. But scientists are already testing solar sails for use in the future. A solar sail is like a large mirror that uses light from the sun and stars. As light hits the sail, it creates a force that drives the sail forward. Spaceships that use solar sails would take longer to gather speed than rocket-propelled ships, but they would eventually go much faster.

Solar sail

To make it possible for humans to live on Mars, we would have to terraform it — make it more like Earth. This could be done in several ways. We could heat up the planet with the use of huge reflective mirrors out in space. We could also introduce bacteria or plants to raise the oxygen level on Mars.

Space shuttle

Terraforming on Mars

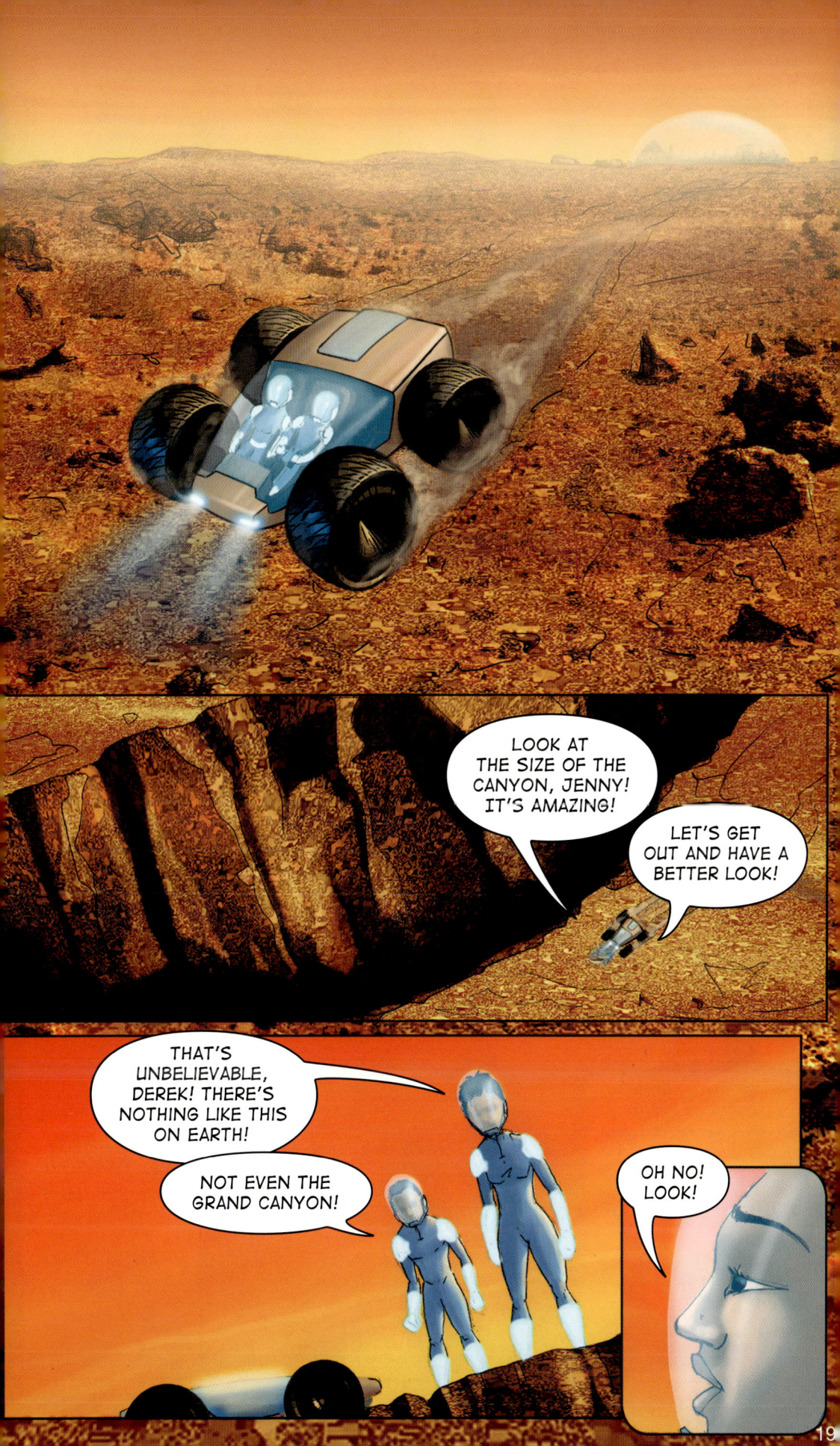

Mars Facts and Figures

Mars is only about half as big as Earth.

Mars is much colder than Earth. The temperature ranges between −225 and +80 degrees Fahrenheit. In comparison, the temperature on Earth ranges from −126 to +136 degrees Fahrenheit.

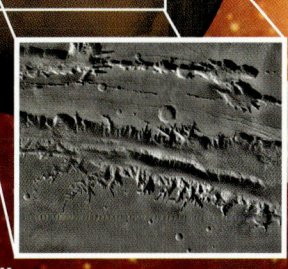

Valles Marineris

Valles Marineris, mentioned in this story, is 2,500 miles long and up to 5 miles deep. The Grand Canyon in the southwestern United States is 277 miles long and 1 mile deep.

A Martian day is about 24 hours and 40 minutes long. A day is the length of time a planet takes to turn around its own axis.

A Martian year is 687 Earth days (an Earth year is 365 days). A year is the length of time a planet takes to move around the sun.

Mars has the largest volcano in the solar system. Called Olympus Mons, it is 15 miles high (Mount Everest is 5.5 miles high).

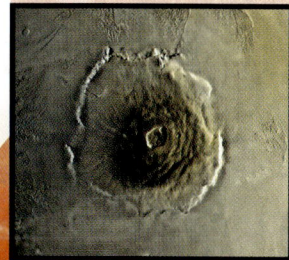

Olympus Mons

Chapter 3: The Rescue

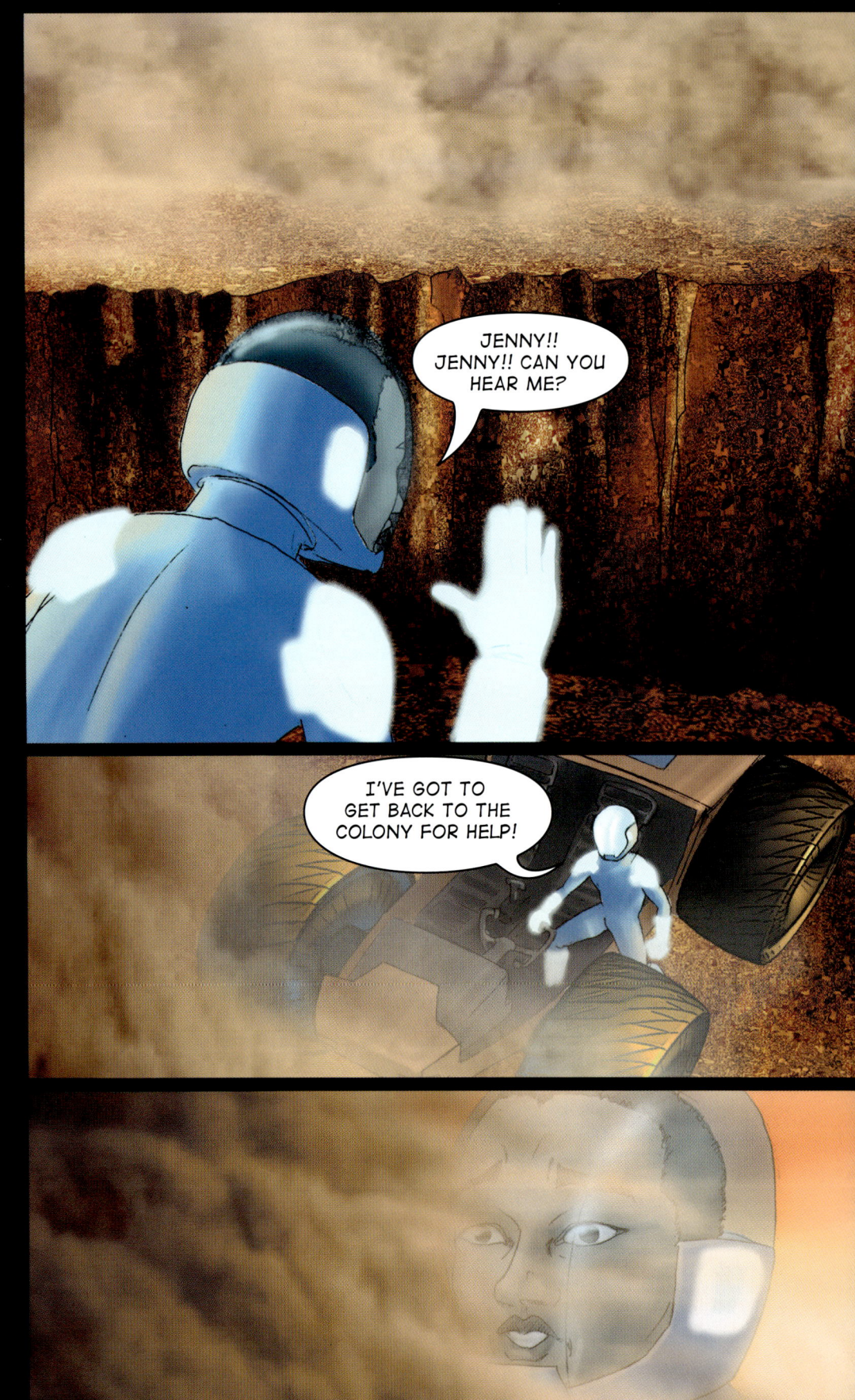

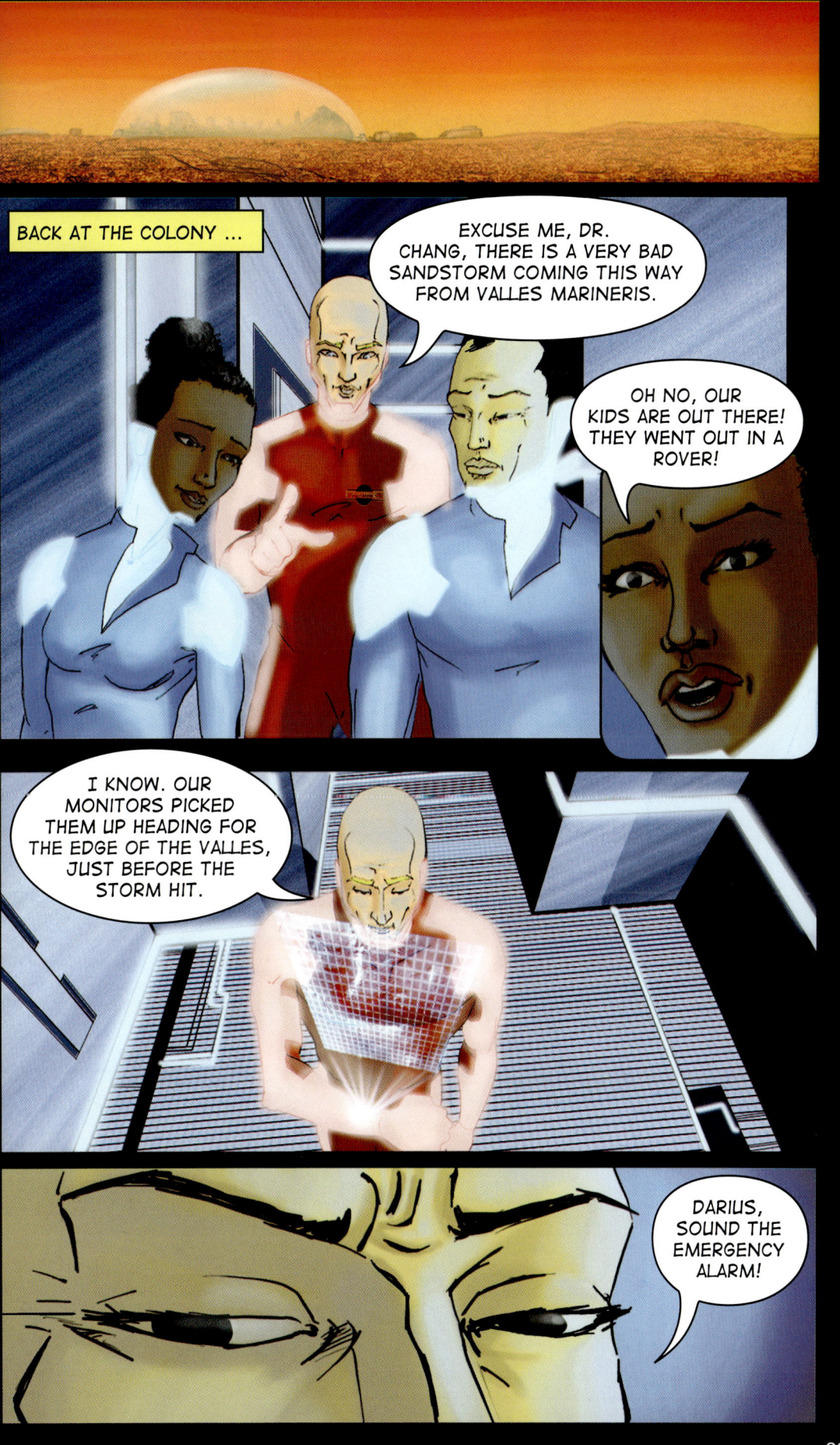

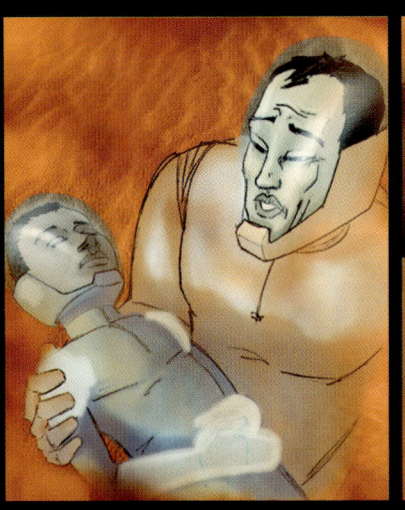

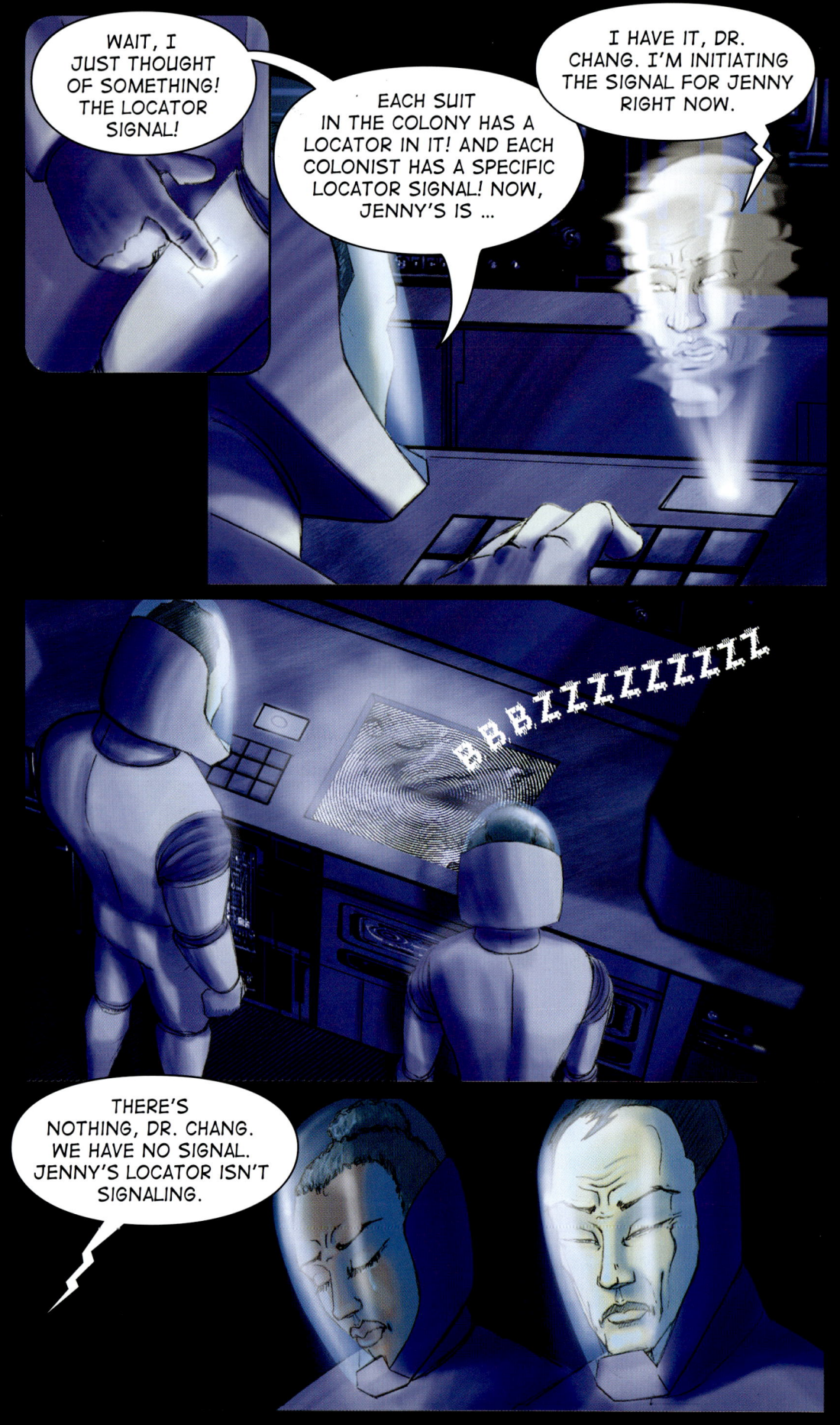

A sandstorm on Mars

Weather on Mars

The weather on Mars can be very severe. The planet sometimes gets hit by huge storms of wind and ice measuring thousands of miles across. There are also dust storms that can last for several months. Some Martian dust storms grow so large that they can cover up the entire planet.

Ice caps on Mars

The surface of Mars is dry and dusty. Temperatures rise and fall very quickly, as in a desert. This helps to create severe weather conditions.

Scientists need to know about the weather on Mars in order to plan when to send space missions there. They get regular reports from space probes that orbit Mars.

Space probe

LIFE ON MARS

TIME OUT!

In 1894, Percival Lowell, a British astronomer, claimed that he could see evidence of life on Mars through his telescope. He was proven wrong.

But in 1996, a meteorite was found in Antarctica. It had landed on Earth 13,000 years ago. Scientists think they have found the preserved remains of microbes — very tiny living things — in this rock. If they are correct, this could mean that life exists — or once existed — on Mars.

Microbes on meteorite

The key to life is water in its liquid form. There is a huge amount of water on Mars, but much of it is ice and the rest is water vapor. It is possible that several million years ago, there was liquid water on Mars that supported life. It is also possible that even now there is liquid water underground or in places we haven't looked yet.

Evidence of water on Mars

Is there life on Mars? We may find nothing when we get there. Or we may be in for a very big surprise.

"OVER THOUSANDS OF YEARS, WE DEVELOPED SPECIAL POWERS THAT ALLOWED US TO MAKE A HOME IN THE VAST CAVERNS THAT MAKE UP OUR PLANET."

KORDOK, SAURNA, WE APOLOGIZE. WE HAD NO IDEA THERE WERE PEOPLE ON MARS ... I MEAN, KAERI. WE WOULD NEVER HAVE TERRAFORMED YOUR PLANET IF WE'D KNOWN.

NO NEED TO APOLOGIZE, DR. CHANG! WE'RE PLEASED AT WHAT YOU'RE DOING. YOU'LL MAKE THE PLANET WHOLE AGAIN ONE DAY!

THERE IS ROOM ENOUGH FOR BOTH OUR CIVILIZATIONS, DR. CHANG. WE ALWAYS KNEW YOU WOULD COME.

YOU SEE, WE'RE RELATED TO YOU!

FAMILIES HAVE A WAY OF ALWAYS RETURNING TO EACH OTHER!

The surface of Mars

TIME OUT!

Exploring Mars

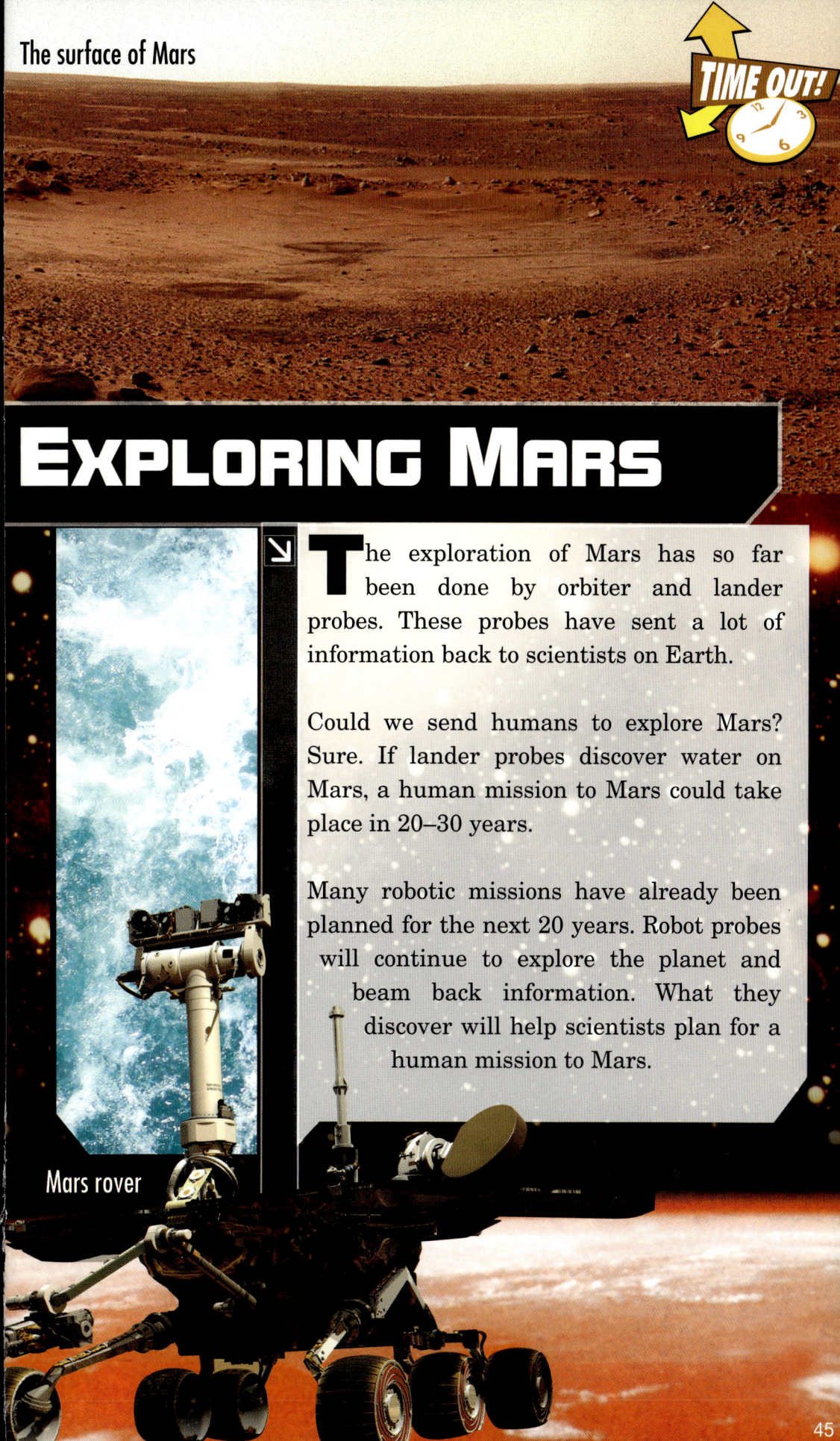
Mars rover

The exploration of Mars has so far been done by orbiter and lander probes. These probes have sent a lot of information back to scientists on Earth.

Could we send humans to explore Mars? Sure. If lander probes discover water on Mars, a human mission to Mars could take place in 20–30 years.

Many robotic missions have already been planned for the next 20 years. Robot probes will continue to explore the planet and beam back information. What they discover will help scientists plan for a human mission to Mars.

Mars in Our

Mars is similar to Earth in many ways. Its day is about as long as ours. It has a hard, rocky surface that we can build on. Mars also has an atmosphere, but it has 200 times less oxygen than ours. Since the first space probes visited in 1964, we have learned a great deal about the red planet. Perhaps, in time, we will learn enough about it to live there.

Mars lander

Future

Space exploration has brought many benefits. In planning for space missions, scientists and engineers have invented many things that we now use in everyday life. Sneakers, cell phones, and satellite television are some items that have been developed with space technology.

Imagine living on Mars! It's an exciting dream! But perhaps we should remind ourselves how lucky we are to live on Earth.

INDEX

A
Antarctica, 4, 37
Atmosphere, 46

C
Chang, Jenny, 7, 9–10, 12, 15, 19–20, 22, 26–28, 30–36, 38, 42, 44
Chang, Derek, 11–12, 19, 26–27, 35–36, 38, 40–41
Chang, Dr. Jean & Michael, 23–24, 26–28, 36, 43
Colony, 6, 9, 12, 14, 16, 22–23, 27–28, 35, 40

D
Darius, John, 16–17, 23–25, 34, 36, 39

E
Earth, 4–6, 12–13, 16, 18–19, 21, 34, 37, 42, 44–47
Everest, 21

G
Grand Canyon, 19, 21

L
Lander, 5, 45
Lowell, Percival, 37

M
Mariner 4, 4–5
Mariner 9, 4
Mars, 4–7, 9–10, 12–14, 16, 21, 29, 37, 40, 45–47
Mercury, 5
Meteorite, 4, 37

Microbes, 37
Moon, 9

O
Olympus Mons, 21
Opportunity, 5

P
Pathfinder, 4
Probes, 29, 45–46

R
Robot, 45
Rover, 5, 10, 18, 23, 25, 45

S
Sandstorm, 20, 23, 26, 29, 31, 34
Satellites, 34, 47
Solar sail, 10–13
Sun, 5, 11

T
Temperature, 21, 29
Terraforming, 10, 13, 43

U
United States, 21

V
Valles Marineris, 14, 21, 23, 33
Venus, 5
Volcano, 21

W
Weather, 29